ULTIMATE
BUDGET

Good Things, Take Time To Grow

Managing Your Budget

YOU HAVE THE DISCIPLINE TO MAKE HARD FINANCIAL CHOICES NOW, TO ENJOY AN EASY LIFE LATER

Calculate your weekly income

List your expenses then break it down by due dates

Create a detail budget

Include saving and Investing in your budget.

SAVINGS ACTION *plan*

GOALS

GOAL PROGRESS: 0% | | | | | | | | | | | 100%

ACTION STEPS

POSSIBLE OBSTACLES

HOW TO OVERCOME OBSTACLES

Debt Tracker

List your debts, then start with the smallest balance using the Snowball Tracker

Smallest Balance	Total Payments

List of Debts	Payment

INCOME

Month:

Date	Source	Expected	Actual
		TOTAL	

Side Hustle

OTHER INCOME

Date	Source	Expected	Actual
		TOTAL	

Monthly Budget Planner

Total Income	

BILLS TO BE PAID	BUDGET	ACTUAL	DIFFERENCE	BILL DUE DATE/NOTES
Budget is balance when Income - Expenses = Zero				
Rent/Mortgage				
Car Payment				
Car Insurance				
Electricity				
Cables				
Gas				
Phone				

\>>>>>

TOTAL BUDGETED	

Other Expenses Budget

Other Expenses and Subscriptions

EXPENSES	BUDGET	ACTUAL	DIFFERENCE	BILL DUE DATE/NOTES

MONTHLY BUDGET SAVINGS GOALS

TOTAL BUDGETED

FUND	BUDGET	ACTUAL
Emergency Fund		
Investment		
Savings		
Auto Repair		

TOTAL BUDGETED

Balance Budget

INCOME TOTAL	BUDGET TOTAL	DIFFERENCE
⊕	⊜	

>>>>>

Monthly Spending *Tracker*

Date	Description	Category	Amount
		Total	

monthly Overview

Sunday	Monday	Tuesday	Wednesday	Thursday	Friday	Saturday

→ **WHAT ARE MY FINANCIAL PRIORITIES THIS MONTH**

→ **WHAT IS MY SELF-CARE GOAL THIS MONTH**

My finances don't scare me because I have a plan

WEEKLY PLANNER

Monday

Tuesday

Wednesday

Thursday

Friday

Saturday

Sunday

GOALS

AFFIRMATION

Meal Planner
STAY ON BUDGET

NOTES

Bill Payment

Weekly Income:

Week of:

This Week Bills Due / Paid Date	Amount Owe	Amount Paid	Full Payment	Partial Payment	Balance Due
			☐	☐	
			☐	☐	
			☐	☐	
			☐	☐	
			☐	☐	
			☐	☐	
			☐	☐	
			☐	☐	
			☐	☐	
			☐	☐	
			☐	☐	

TOTAL PAID: **TOTAL DUE:**

Notes / Unexpected Expenses:

WEEKLY PLANNER

Monday

Tuesday

Wednesday

Thursday

Friday

Saturday

Sunday

GOALS

AFFIRMATION

Meal Planner
STAY ON BUDGET

NOTES

Bill Payment

Weekly Income:

Week of:

This Week Bills Due / Paid Date	Amount Owe	Amount Paid	Full Payment	Partial Payment	Balance Due
			☐	☐	
			☐	☐	
			☐	☐	
			☐	☐	
			☐	☐	
			☐	☐	
			☐	☐	
			☐	☐	
			☐	☐	
			☐	☐	
			☐	☐	

TOTAL PAID: **TOTAL DUE:**

Notes / Unexpected Expenses:

WEEKLY PLANNER

Monday

Tuesday

Wednesday

Thursday

Friday

Saturday

Sunday

GOALS

AFFIRMATION

Meal Planner
STAY ON BUDGET

NOTES

Bill Payment

Weekly Income: _____

Week of: _____

This Week Bills Due / Paid Date	Amount Owe	Amount Paid	Full Payment	Partial Payment	Balance Due
			☐	☐	
			☐	☐	
			☐	☐	
			☐	☐	
			☐	☐	
			☐	☐	
			☐	☐	
			☐	☐	
			☐	☐	
			☐	☐	
			☐	☐	

TOTAL PAID: _____ **TOTAL DUE:** _____

Notes / Unexpected Expenses:

_____

_____

_____   _____

_____   _____

_____   _____

_____   _____

_____   _____

WEEKLY PLANNER

Monday

Tuesday

Wednesday

Thursday

Friday

Saturday

Sunday

GOALS

AFFIRMATION

Meal Planner

STAY ON BUDGET

NOTES

Bill Payment

Weekly Income:

Week of: _____

This Week Bills Due / Paid Date	Amount Owe	Amount Paid	Full Payment	Partial Payment	Balance Due
			☐	☐	
			☐	☐	
			☐	☐	
			☐	☐	
			☐	☐	
			☐	☐	
			☐	☐	
			☐	☐	
			☐	☐	
			☐	☐	
			☐	☐	
	TOTAL PAID:			**TOTAL DUE:**	

Notes / Unexpected Expenses:

_____

_____

_____

_____

_____

_____

Reflections

monthly Review

DOES MY INCOME AND DEBT ADD UP

_____

_____

_____

HOW CAN I MAKE NEXT MONTH BETTER

_____

_____

WHAT DID I LEARN THIS MONTH ABOUT MY
SPENDING

_____

_____

_____

DO I NEED TO ADJUST
SPENDING LIMITS

_____

_____

_____

DID MEET THIS MONTH'S
GOALS

INCOME

Month:

Date	Source	Expected	Actual
		TOTAL	

Side Hustle

OTHER INCOME

Date	Source	Expected	Actual
		TOTAL	

<<<<<

Total Income	

BILLS TO BE PAID	BUDGET	ACTUAL	DIFFERENCE	BILL DUE DATE/NOTES
Budget is balance when Income - Expenses = Zero				
Rent/Mortgage				
Car Payment				
Car Insurance				
Electricity				
Cables				
Gas				
Phone				

>>>>>

TOTAL BUDGETED	

Other Expenses Budget

〈〈〈〈〈

Other Expenses and Subscriptions

EXPENSES	BUDGET	ACTUAL	DIFFERENCE	BILL DUE DATE/NOTES

TOTAL BUDGETED

MONTHLY BUDGET SAVINGS GOALS

FUND	BUDGET	ACTUAL
Emergency Fund		
Investment		
Savings		
Auto Repair		

TOTAL BUDGETED

Balance Budget

〉〉〉〉〉

INCOME TOTAL	BUDGET TOTAL	DIFFERENCE
⊕	⊜	

Monthly Spending *Tracker*

Date	Description	Category	Amount
		Total	

CALENDAR

monthly Overview

Sunday	Monday	Tuesday	Wednesday	Thursday	Friday	Saturday

⌐→ WHAT ARE MY FINANCIAL
PRIORITIES THIS MONTH

⌐→ WHAT IS MY SELF-CARE
GOAL THIS MONTH

My finances don't scare me because I have a plan

WEEKLY PLANNER

Monday

Tuesday

Wednesday

Thursday

Friday

Saturday

Sunday

GOALS

AFFIRMATION

Meal Planner

STAY ON BUDGET

NOTES

Bill Payment

Weekly Income:

Week of: _____

This Week Bills Due / Paid Date	Amount Owe	Amount Paid	Full Payment	Partial Payment	Balance Due
			▢	▢	
			▢	▢	
			▢	▢	
			▢	▢	
			▢	▢	
			▢	▢	
			▢	▢	
			▢	▢	
			▢	▢	
			▢	▢	
			▢	▢	
	TOTAL PAID:			TOTAL DUE:	

Notes / Unexpected Expenses:

_____

_____

_____   _____

_____   _____

_____   _____

_____   _____

_____

WEEKLY PLANNER

Monday

Tuesday

Wednesday

Thursday

Friday

Saturday

Sunday

GOALS

AFFIRMATION

Meal Planner

STAY ON BUDGET

NOTES

Bill Payment

Weekly Income:

Week of: _____

This Week Bills Due / Paid Date	Amount Owe	Amount Paid	Full Payment	Partial Payment	Balance Due
			☐	☐	
			☐	☐	
			☐	☐	
			☐	☐	
			☐	☐	
			☐	☐	
			☐	☐	
			☐	☐	
			☐	☐	
			☐	☐	
			☐	☐	

TOTAL PAID: _____ **TOTAL DUE:** _____

Notes / Unexpected Expenses:

_____

_____

_____ _____

_____ _____

_____ _____

_____ _____

WEEKLY PLANNER

Monday

Tuesday

Wednesday

Thursday

Friday

Saturday

Sunday

GOALS

AFFIRMATION

Meal Planner

STAY ON BUDGET

NOTES

Bill Payment

Weekly Income:

Week of: _____

This Week Bills Due / Paid Date	Amount Owe	Amount Paid	Full Payment	Partial Payment	Balance Due
			☐	☐	
			☐	☐	
			☐	☐	
			☐	☐	
			☐	☐	
			☐	☐	
			☐	☐	
			☐	☐	
			☐	☐	
			☐	☐	
			☐	☐	
	TOTAL PAID:			**TOTAL DUE:**	

Notes / Unexpected Expenses:

_____

_____

_____   _____

_____   _____

_____   _____

_____

WEEKLY PLANNER

Monday

Tuesday

Wednesday

Thursday

Friday

Saturday

Sunday

GOALS

AFFIRMATION

Meal Planner

STAY ON BUDGET

NOTES

Bill Payment

Weekly Income:

Week of: _____

This Week Bills Due / Paid Date	Amount Owe	Amount Paid	Full Payment	Partial Payment	Balance Due
			☐	☐	
			☐	☐	
			☐	☐	
			☐	☐	
			☐	☐	
			☐	☐	
			☐	☐	
			☐	☐	
			☐	☐	
			☐	☐	
			☐	☐	

TOTAL PAID: _____   **TOTAL DUE:** _____

Notes / Unexpected Expenses:

_____

_____

_____   _____

_____   _____

_____   _____

_____   _____

Reflections

monthly Review

DOES MY INCOME AND DEBT ADD UP

_____

_____

_____

HOW CAN I MAKE NEXT MONTH BETTER

_____

_____

WHAT DID I LEARN THIS MONTH ABOUT MY
SPENDING

_____

_____

_____

DO I NEED TO ADJUST
SPENDING LIMITS

_____

_____

_____

DID MEET THIS MONTH'S
GOALS

INCOME

Month:

Date	Source	Expected	Actual
		TOTAL	

Side Hustle

OTHER INCOME

Date	Source	Expected	Actual
		TOTAL	

Monthly Budget Planner

<<<<<

Total Income	

BILLS TO BE PAID	BUDGET	ACTUAL	DIFFERENCE	BILL DUE DATE/NOTES
Budget is balance when Income - Expenses = Zero				
Rent/Mortgage				
Car Payment				
Car Insurance				
Electricity				
Cables				
Gas				
Phone				

>>>>>

TOTAL BUDGETED	

Other Expenses Budget

Other Expenses and Subscriptions

EXPENSES	BUDGET	ACTUAL	DIFFERENCE	BILL DUE DATE/NOTES

MONTHLY BUDGET SAVINGS GOALS

TOTAL BUDGETED

FUND	BUDGET	ACTUAL
Emergency Fund		
Investment		
Savings		
Auto Repair		

TOTAL BUDGETED

Balance Budget

INCOME TOTAL	BUDGET TOTAL	DIFFERENCE
	⊕	⊜

»»»

Monthly Spending *Tracker*

Date	Description	Category	Amount
		Total	

CALENDAR

monthly Overview

Sunday	Monday	Tuesday	Wednesday	Thursday	Friday	Saturday

↳ WHAT ARE MY FINANCIAL
PRIORITIES THIS MONTH

↳ WHAT IS MY SELF-CARE
GOAL THIS MONTH

My finances don't scare me because I have a plan

WEEKLY PLANNER

Monday

Tuesday

Wednesday

Thursday

Friday

Saturday

Sunday

GOALS

AFFIRMATION

Meal Planner
STAY ON BUDGET

NOTES

Bill Payment

Weekly Income:

Week of:

This Week Bills Due / Paid Date	Amount Owe	Amount Paid	Full Payment	Partial Payment	Balance Due

TOTAL PAID: **TOTAL DUE:**

Notes / Unexpected Expenses:

_____

_____

_____ _____

_____ _____

_____ _____

_____ _____

_____

WEEKLY PLANNER

Monday

Tuesday

Wednesday

Thursday

Friday

Saturday

Sunday

GOALS

AFFIRMATION

Meal Planner
STAY ON BUDGET

NOTES

Bill Payment

Weekly Income:

Week of:

This Week Bills Due / Paid Date	Amount Owe	Amount Paid	Full Payment	Partial Payment	Balance Due
			☐	☐	
			☐	☐	
			☐	☐	
			☐	☐	
			☐	☐	
			☐	☐	
			☐	☐	
			☐	☐	
			☐	☐	
			☐	☐	
			☐	☐	

TOTAL PAID: | | **TOTAL DUE:** |

Notes / Unexpected Expenses:

WEEKLY PLANNER

Monday

Tuesday

Wednesday

Thursday

Friday

Saturday

Sunday

GOALS

AFFIRMATION

Meal Planner
STAY ON BUDGET

NOTES

Bill Payment

Weekly Income:

Week of: _____

This Week Bills Due / Paid Date	Amount Owe	Amount Paid	Full Payment	Partial Payment	Balance Due
			☐	☐	
			☐	☐	
			☐	☐	
			☐	☐	
			☐	☐	
			☐	☐	
			☐	☐	
			☐	☐	
			☐	☐	
			☐	☐	
			☐	☐	
	TOTAL PAID:			**TOTAL DUE:**	

Notes / Unexpected Expenses:

_____

_____

_____   _____

_____   _____

_____   _____

_____   _____

_____

WEEKLY PLANNER

Monday

Tuesday

Wednesday

Thursday

Friday

Saturday

Sunday

GOALS

AFFIRMATION

Meal Planner
STAY ON BUDGET

NOTES

Bill Payment

Weekly Income:

Week of:

This Week Bills Due / Paid Date	Amount Owe	Amount Paid	Full Payment	Partial Payment	Balance Due
			▢	▢	
			▢	▢	
			▢	▢	
			▢	▢	
			▢	▢	
			▢	▢	
			▢	▢	
			▢	▢	
			▢	▢	
			▢	▢	
			▢	▢	

TOTAL PAID: **TOTAL DUE:**

Notes / Unexpected Expenses:

_____

_____

_____   _____

_____   _____

_____   _____

_____   _____

Reflections

monthly Review

DOES MY INCOME AND DEBT ADD UP

_____

_____

_____

HOW CAN I MAKE NEXT MONTH BETTER

_____

_____

WHAT DID I LEARN THIS MONTH ABOUT MY
SPENDING

_____

_____

_____

DO I NEED TO ADJUST
SPENDING LIMITS

_____

_____

_____

DID MEET THIS MONTH'S
GOALS

INCOME

Month:

Date	Source	Expected	Actual
		TOTAL	

Side Hustle

OTHER INCOME

Date	Source	Expected	Actual
		TOTAL	

Monthly Budget Planner

<<<<<

Total Income	

BILLS TO BE PAID	BUDGET	ACTUAL	DIFFERENCE	BILL DUE DATE/NOTES
Budget is balance when Income - Expenses = Zero				
Rent/Mortgage				
Car Payment				
Car Insurance				
Electricity				
Cables				
Gas				
Phone				

>>>>>

TOTAL BUDGETED	

Other Expenses Budget

Other Expenses and Subscriptions

EXPENSES	BUDGET	ACTUAL	DIFFERENCE	BILL DUE DATE/NOTES

TOTAL BUDGETED

MONTHLY BUDGET SAVINGS GOALS

FUND	BUDGET	ACTUAL
Emergency Fund		
Investment		
Savings		
Auto Repair		

TOTAL BUDGETED

Balance Budget

INCOME TOTAL	BUDGET TOTAL	DIFFERENCE
⊕	⊜	

>>>>>

Monthly Spending *Tracker*

Date	Description	Category	Amount
		Total	

monthly Overview

Sunday	Monday	Tuesday	Wednesday	Thursday	Friday	Saturday

⟶ WHAT ARE MY FINANCIAL
PRIORITIES THIS MONTH

⟶ WHAT IS MY SELF-CARE
GOAL THIS MONTH

My finances don't scare me because I have a plan

WEEKLY PLANNER

Monday

Tuesday

Wednesday

Thursday

Friday

Saturday

Sunday

GOALS

AFFIRMATION

Meal Planner
STAY ON BUDGET

NOTES

Bill Payment

Weekly Income:

Week of:

This Week Bills Due / Paid Date	Amount Owe	Amount Paid	Full Payment	Partial Payment	Balance Due
			☐	☐	
			☐	☐	
			☐	☐	
			☐	☐	
			☐	☐	
			☐	☐	
			☐	☐	
			☐	☐	
			☐	☐	
			☐	☐	
			☐	☐	

TOTAL PAID: | **TOTAL DUE:**

Notes / Unexpected Expenses:

WEEKLY PLANNER

Monday

Tuesday

Wednesday

Thursday

Friday

Saturday

Sunday

GOALS

AFFIRMATION

Meal Planner

STAY ON BUDGET

NOTES

Bill Payment

Weekly Income:

Week of: _____

This Week Bills Due / Paid Date	Amount Owe	Amount Paid	Full Payment	Partial Payment	Balance Due

TOTAL PAID:		TOTAL DUE:	

Notes / Unexpected Expenses:

_____

_____

_____ _____

_____ _____

_____ _____

_____ _____

_____

WEEKLY PLANNER

Monday

Tuesday

Wednesday

Thursday

Friday

Saturday

Sunday

GOALS

AFFIRMATION

Meal Planner
STAY ON BUDGET

NOTES

Bill Payment

Weekly Income:

Week of:

This Week Bills Due / Paid Date	Amount Owe	Amount Paid	Full Payment	Partial Payment	Balance Due
			☐	☐	
			☐	☐	
			☐	☐	
			☐	☐	
			☐	☐	
			☐	☐	
			☐	☐	
			☐	☐	
			☐	☐	
			☐	☐	
			☐	☐	

| | TOTAL PAID: | | | TOTAL DUE: | |

Notes / Unexpected Expenses:

_____

_____

_____   _____

_____   _____

_____   _____

_____   _____

_____

WEEKLY PLANNER

Monday

Tuesday

Wednesday

Thursday

Friday

Saturday

Sunday

GOALS

AFFIRMATION

Meal Planner
STAY ON BUDGET

NOTES

Bill Payment

Weekly Income:

Week of: _____

This Week Bills Due / Paid Date	Amount Owe	Amount Paid	Full Payment	Partial Payment	Balance Due
			☐	☐	
			☐	☐	
			☐	☐	
			☐	☐	
			☐	☐	
			☐	☐	
			☐	☐	
			☐	☐	
			☐	☐	
			☐	☐	
			☐	☐	

TOTAL PAID: _____   **TOTAL DUE:** _____

Notes / Unexpected Expenses:

_____

_____

_____   _____

_____   _____

_____   _____

_____   _____

_____   _____

_____

Reflections

monthly Review

DOES MY INCOME AND DEBT ADD UP

_____

_____

_____

HOW CAN I MAKE NEXT MONTH BETTER

_____

_____

WHAT DID I LEARN THIS MONTH ABOUT MY
SPENDING

_____

_____

_____

DO I NEED TO ADJUST
SPENDING LIMITS

_____

_____

_____

DID MEET THIS MONTH'S
GOALS

INCOME

Month:

Date	Source	Expected	Actual
		TOTAL	

Side Hustle

OTHER INCOME

Date	Source	Expected	Actual
		TOTAL	

<<<<<

Total Income	

BILLS TO BE PAID	BUDGET	ACTUAL	DIFFERENCE	BILL DUE DATE/NOTES
Budget is balance when Income - Expenses = Zero				
Rent/Mortgage				
Car Payment				
Car Insurance				
Electricity				
Cables				
Gas				
Phone				

>>>>>

TOTAL BUDGETED	

Other Expenses and Subscriptions

EXPENSES	BUDGET	ACTUAL	DIFFERENCE	BILL DUE DATE/NOTES

MONTHLY BUDGET SAVINGS GOALS

TOTAL BUDGETED

FUND	BUDGET	ACTUAL
Emergency Fund		
Investment		
Savings		
Auto Repair		

TOTAL BUDGETED

Balance

Budget

>>>>>	INCOME TOTAL	BUDGET TOTAL	DIFFERENCE
	⊕	⊜	

Monthly Spending Tracker

Date	Description	Category	Amount
		Total	

monthly Overview

Sunday	Monday	Tuesday	Wednesday	Thursday	Friday	Saturday

⮕ WHAT ARE MY FINANCIAL
PRIORITIES THIS MONTH

⮕ WHAT IS MY SELF-CARE
GOAL THIS MONTH

My finances don't scare me because I have a plan

WEEKLY PLANNER

Monday

Tuesday

Wednesday

Thursday

Friday

Saturday

Sunday

GOALS

AFFIRMATION

Meal Planner

S T A Y   O N   B U D G E T

NOTES

Bill Payment

Weekly Income:

Week of: _____

This Week Bills Due / Paid Date	Amount Owe	Amount Paid	Full Payment	Partial Payment	Balance Due
			☐	☐	
			☐	☐	
			☐	☐	
			☐	☐	
			☐	☐	
			☐	☐	
			☐	☐	
			☐	☐	
			☐	☐	
			☐	☐	
			☐	☐	

TOTAL PAID: _____   **TOTAL DUE:** _____

Notes / Unexpected Expenses:

_____

_____

_____   _____

_____   _____

_____   _____

_____   _____

WEEKLY PLANNER

Monday

Tuesday

Wednesday

Thursday

Friday

Saturday

Sunday

GOALS

AFFIRMATION

Meal Planner

STAY ON BUDGET

NOTES

Bill Payment

Weekly Income:

Week of:

This Week Bills Due / Paid Date	Amount Owe	Amount Paid	Full Payment	Partial Payment	Balance Due
			☐	☐	
			☐	☐	
			☐	☐	
			☐	☐	
			☐	☐	
			☐	☐	
			☐	☐	
			☐	☐	
			☐	☐	
			☐	☐	
			☐	☐	

TOTAL PAID: | **TOTAL DUE:**

Notes / Unexpected Expenses:

WEEKLY PLANNER

Monday

Tuesday

Wednesday

Thursday

Friday

Saturday

Sunday

GOALS

AFFIRMATION

Meal Planner
STAY ON BUDGET

NOTES

Bill Payment

Weekly Income:

Week of: _____

This Week Bills Due / Paid Date	Amount Owe	Amount Paid	Full Payment	Partial Payment	Balance Due
			☐	☐	
			☐	☐	
			☐	☐	
			☐	☐	
			☐	☐	
			☐	☐	
			☐	☐	
			☐	☐	
			☐	☐	
			☐	☐	
			☐	☐	
	TOTAL PAID:			**TOTAL DUE:**	

Notes / Unexpected Expenses:

_____

_____

_____   _____

_____   _____

_____   _____

_____   _____

WEEKLY PLANNER

Monday

Tuesday

Wednesday

Thursday

Friday

Saturday

Sunday

GOALS

AFFIRMATION

Meal Planner

STAY ON BUDGET

NOTES

Bill Payment

Weekly Income:

Week of: _____

This Week Bills Due / Paid Date	Amount Owe	Amount Paid	Full Payment	Partial Payment	Balance Due
			☐	☐	
			☐	☐	
			☐	☐	
			☐	☐	
			☐	☐	
			☐	☐	
			☐	☐	
			☐	☐	
			☐	☐	
			☐	☐	
			☐	☐	

TOTAL PAID: _____   **TOTAL DUE:** _____

Notes / Unexpected Expenses:

_____

_____

_____   _____

_____   _____

_____   _____

_____   _____

Reflections

monthly Review

DOES MY INCOME AND DEBT ADD UP

_____

_____

_____

HOW CAN I MAKE NEXT MONTH BETTER

_____

_____

WHAT DID I LEARN THIS MONTH ABOUT MY SPENDING

_____

_____

_____

DO I NEED TO ADJUST
SPENDING LIMITS

_____

_____

_____

DID MEET THIS MONTH'S
GOALS

INCOME

Month:

Date	Source	Expected	Actual
		TOTAL	

Side Hustle

OTHER INCOME

Date	Source	Expected	Actual
		TOTAL	

Monthly Budget Planner

‹‹‹‹‹

Total Income	

BILLS TO BE PAID	BUDGET	ACTUAL	DIFFERENCE	BILL DUE DATE/NOTES
Budget is balance when Income - Expenses = Zero				
Rent/Mortgage				
Car Payment				
Car Insurance				
Electricity				
Cables				
Gas				
Phone				

››››› | TOTAL BUDGETED | |

Other Expenses Budget

Other Expenses and Subscriptions

EXPENSES	BUDGET	ACTUAL	DIFFERENCE	BILL DUE DATE/NOTES

TOTAL BUDGETED

MONTHLY BUDGET SAVINGS GOALS

FUND	BUDGET	ACTUAL
Emergency Fund		
Investment		
Savings		
Auto Repair		

TOTAL BUDGETED

Balance Budget

INCOME TOTAL	BUDGET TOTAL	DIFFERENCE
⊕	⊜	

Monthly Spending *Tracker*

Date	Description	Category	Amount
		Total	

CALENDAR

monthly Overview

Sunday	Monday	Tuesday	Wednesday	Thursday	Friday	Saturday

↳ WHAT ARE MY FINANCIAL PRIORITIES THIS MONTH

↳ WHAT IS MY SELF-CARE GOAL THIS MONTH

My finances don't scare me because I have a plan

WEEKLY PLANNER

Monday

Tuesday

Wednesday

Thursday

Friday

Saturday

Sunday

GOALS

AFFIRMATION

Meal Planner

STAY ON BUDGET

NOTES

Bill Payment

Weekly Income:

Week of:

This Week Bills Due / Paid Date	Amount Owe	Amount Paid	Full Payment	Partial Payment	Balance Due
			☐	☐	
			☐	☐	
			☐	☐	
			☐	☐	
			☐	☐	
			☐	☐	
			☐	☐	
			☐	☐	
			☐	☐	
			☐	☐	
			☐	☐	

TOTAL PAID: | **TOTAL DUE:**

Notes / Unexpected Expenses:

_____

_____

_____   _____

_____   _____

_____   _____

_____   _____

_____

WEEKLY PLANNER

Monday

Tuesday

Wednesday

Thursday

Friday

Saturday

Sunday

GOALS

AFFIRMATION

Meal Planner

STAY ON BUDGET

NOTES

Bill Payment

Weekly Income:

Week of:

This Week Bills Due / Paid Date	Amount Owe	Amount Paid	Full Payment	Partial Payment	Balance Due
			☐	☐	
			☐	☐	
			☐	☐	
			☐	☐	
			☐	☐	
			☐	☐	
			☐	☐	
			☐	☐	
			☐	☐	
			☐	☐	
			☐	☐	

TOTAL PAID: **TOTAL DUE:**

Notes / Unexpected Expenses:

WEEKLY PLANNER

Monday

Tuesday

Wednesday

Thursday

Friday

Saturday

Sunday

GOALS

AFFIRMATION

Meal Planner

STAY ON BUDGET

NOTES

Bill Payment

Weekly Income:

Week of: _____

This Week Bills Due / Paid Date	Amount Owe	Amount Paid	Full Payment	Partial Payment	Balance Due
			☐	☐	
			☐	☐	
			☐	☐	
			☐	☐	
			☐	☐	
			☐	☐	
			☐	☐	
			☐	☐	
			☐	☐	
			☐	☐	
			☐	☐	
	TOTAL PAID:			**TOTAL DUE:**	

Notes / Unexpected Expenses:

WEEKLY PLANNER

Monday

Tuesday

Wednesday

Thursday

Friday

Saturday

Sunday

GOALS

AFFIRMATION

Meal Planner
STAY ON BUDGET

NOTES

Bill Payment

Weekly Income:

Week of:

This Week Bills Due / Paid Date	Amount Owe	Amount Paid	Full Payment	Partial Payment	Balance Due
			☐	☐	
			☐	☐	
			☐	☐	
			☐	☐	
			☐	☐	
			☐	☐	
			☐	☐	
			☐	☐	
			☐	☐	
			☐	☐	
			☐	☐	

TOTAL PAID: | **TOTAL DUE:**

Notes / Unexpected Expenses:

_____

_____

_____ _____

_____ _____

_____ _____

_____ _____

_____

Reflections

monthly Review

DOES MY INCOME AND DEBT ADD UP

_____

_____

_____

HOW CAN I MAKE NEXT MONTH BETTER

_____

_____

WHAT DID I LEARN THIS MONTH ABOUT MY
SPENDING

_____

_____

_____

DO I NEED TO ADJUST
SPENDING LIMITS

_____

_____

_____

DID MEET THIS MONTH'S
GOALS

INCOME

Month:

Date	Source	Expected	Actual
		TOTAL	

Side Hustle

OTHER INCOME

Date	Source	Expected	Actual
		TOTAL	

Monthly Budget Planner

Total Income	

BILLS TO BE PAID	BUDGET	ACTUAL	DIFFERENCE	BILL DUE DATE/NOTES
Budget is balance when Income - Expenses = Zero				
Rent/Mortgage				
Car Payment				
Car Insurance				
Electricity				
Cables				
Gas				
Phone				

>>>>>

TOTAL BUDGETED	

Other Expenses Budget

Other Expenses and Subscriptions

EXPENSES	BUDGET	ACTUAL	DIFFERENCE	BILL DUE DATE/NOTES

MONTHLY BUDGET SAVINGS GOALS

TOTAL BUDGETED

FUND	BUDGET	ACTUAL
Emergency Fund		
Investment		
Savings		
Auto Repair		

TOTAL BUDGETED

Balance Budget

	INCOME TOTAL	BUDGET TOTAL	DIFFERENCE
»»»	⊕	⊜	

Monthly Spending *Tracker*

Date	Description	Category	Amount
		Total	

CALENDAR

monthly Overview

Sunday	Monday	Tuesday	Wednesday	Thursday	Friday	Saturday

⟶ WHAT ARE MY FINANCIAL
PRIORITIES THIS MONTH

⟶ WHAT IS MY SELF-CARE
GOAL THIS MONTH

My finances don't scare me because I have a plan

WEEKLY PLANNER

Monday

Tuesday

Wednesday

Thursday

Friday

Saturday

Sunday

GOALS

AFFIRMATION

Meal Planner
STAY ON BUDGET

NOTES

Bill Payment

Weekly Income:

Week of: _____

This Week Bills Due / Paid Date	Amount Owe	Amount Paid	Full Payment	Partial Payment	Balance Due

TOTAL PAID: _____ **TOTAL DUE:** _____

Notes / Unexpected Expenses:

_____

_____

_____ _____

_____ _____

_____ _____

_____ _____

_____

WEEKLY PLANNER

Monday

Tuesday

Wednesday

Thursday

Friday

Saturday

Sunday

GOALS

AFFIRMATION

Meal Planner

STAY ON BUDGET

NOTES

Bill Payment

Weekly Income:

Week of:

This Week Bills Due / Paid Date	Amount Owe	Amount Paid	Full Payment	Partial Payment	Balance Due
			▢	▢	
			▢	▢	
			▢	▢	
			▢	▢	
			▢	▢	
			▢	▢	
			▢	▢	
			▢	▢	
			▢	▢	
			▢	▢	
			▢	▢	

TOTAL PAID: | | **TOTAL DUE:** |

Notes / Unexpected Expenses:

_____

_____

_____   _____

_____   _____

_____   _____

_____   _____

_____   _____

WEEKLY PLANNER

Monday

Tuesday

Wednesday

Thursday

Friday

Saturday

Sunday

GOALS

AFFIRMATION

Meal Planner

STAY ON BUDGET

NOTES

Bill Payment

Weekly Income:

Week of:

This Week Bills Due / Paid Date	Amount Owe	Amount Paid	Full Payment	Partial Payment	Balance Due
			☐	☐	
			☐	☐	
			☐	☐	
			☐	☐	
			☐	☐	
			☐	☐	
			☐	☐	
			☐	☐	
			☐	☐	
			☐	☐	
			☐	☐	

TOTAL PAID: **TOTAL DUE:**

Notes / Unexpected Expenses:

WEEKLY PLANNER

Monday

Tuesday

Wednesday

Thursday

Friday

Saturday

Sunday

GOALS

AFFIRMATION

Meal Planner

STAY ON BUDGET

NOTES

Bill Payment

Weekly Income:

Week of:

This Week Bills Due / Paid Date	Amount Owe	Amount Paid	Full Payment	Partial Payment	Balance Due
	TOTAL PAID:			**TOTAL DUE:**	

Notes / Unexpected Expenses:

_____

_____

_____   _____

_____   _____

_____   _____

_____   _____

Reflections

monthly Review

DOES MY INCOME AND DEBT ADD UP

_____

_____

_____

HOW CAN I MAKE NEXT MONTH BETTER

_____

_____

WHAT DID I LEARN THIS MONTH ABOUT MY
SPENDING

_____

_____

_____

DO I NEED TO ADJUST
SPENDING LIMITS

_____

_____

_____

DID MEET THIS MONTH'S
GOALS

INCOME

Month:

Date	Source	Expected	Actual
		TOTAL	

Side Hustle

OTHER INCOME

Date	Source	Expected	Actual
		TOTAL	

Monthly Budget Planner

<<<<<

Total Income	

BILLS TO BE PAID	BUDGET	ACTUAL	DIFFERENCE	BILL DUE DATE/NOTES
Budget is balance when Income - Expenses = Zero				
Rent/Mortgage				
Car Payment				
Car Insurance				
Electricity				
Cables				
Gas				
Phone				

>>>>>

TOTAL BUDGETED	

Other Expenses Budget

Other Expenses and Subscriptions

EXPENSES	BUDGET	ACTUAL	DIFFERENCE	BILL DUE DATE/NOTES

	TOTAL BUDGETED	

MONTHLY BUDGET SAVINGS GOALS

FUND	BUDGET	ACTUAL
Emergency Fund		
Investment		
Savings		
Auto Repair		

TOTAL BUDGETED	

Balance Budget

INCOME TOTAL	BUDGET TOTAL	DIFFERENCE
⊕	⊜	

Monthly Spending *Tracker*

Date	Description	Category	Amount
		Total	

monthly Overview

Sunday	Monday	Tuesday	Wednesday	Thursday	Friday	Saturday

⟶ WHAT ARE MY FINANCIAL
PRIORITIES THIS MONTH

⟶ WHAT IS MY SELF-CARE
GOAL THIS MONTH

My finances don't scare me because I have a plan

WEEKLY PLANNER

Monday

Tuesday

Wednesday

Thursday

Friday

Saturday

Sunday

GOALS

AFFIRMATION

Meal Planner

STAY ON BUDGET

NOTES

Bill Payment

Weekly Income:

Week of:

This Week Bills Due / Paid Date	Amount Owe	Amount Paid	Full Payment	Partial Payment	Balance Due
			■	■	
			■	■	
			■	■	
			■	■	
			■	■	
			■	■	
			■	■	
			■	■	
			■	■	
			■	■	
			■	■	

TOTAL PAID: **TOTAL DUE:**

Notes / Unexpected Expenses:

_____

_____

_____   _____

_____   _____

_____   _____

_____   _____

WEEKLY PLANNER

Monday

Tuesday

Wednesday

Thursday

Friday

Saturday

Sunday

GOALS

AFFIRMATION

Meal Planner

STAY ON BUDGET

NOTES

Weekly Income:

Bill Payment

Week of:

This Week Bills Due / Paid Date	Amount Owe	Amount Paid	Full Payment	Partial Payment	Balance Due
			▪	▪	
			▪	▪	
			▪	▪	
			▪	▪	
			▪	▪	
			▪	▪	
			▪	▪	
			▪	▪	
			▪	▪	
			▪	▪	
			▪	▪	

TOTAL PAID: **TOTAL DUE:**

Notes / Unexpected Expenses:

WEEKLY PLANNER

Monday

Tuesday

Wednesday

Thursday

Friday

Saturday

Sunday

GOALS

AFFIRMATION

Meal Planner

STAY ON BUDGET

NOTES

Bill Payment

Weekly Income:

Week of: _____

This Week Bills Due / Paid Date	Amount Owe	Amount Paid	Full Payment	Partial Payment	Balance Due
			☐	☐	
			☐	☐	
			☐	☐	
			☐	☐	
			☐	☐	
			☐	☐	
			☐	☐	
			☐	☐	
			☐	☐	
			☐	☐	
			☐	☐	

TOTAL PAID:		TOTAL DUE:	

Notes / Unexpected Expenses:

_____

_____

_____   _____

_____   _____

_____   _____

_____   _____

_____   _____

WEEKLY PLANNER

Monday

Tuesday

Wednesday

Thursday

Friday

Saturday

Sunday

GOALS

AFFIRMATION

Meal Planner
STAY ON BUDGET

NOTES

Bill Payment

Weekly Income:

Week of:

This Week Bills Due / Paid Date	Amount Owe	Amount Paid	Full Payment	Partial Payment	Balance Due
			☐	☐	
			☐	☐	
			☐	☐	
			☐	☐	
			☐	☐	
			☐	☐	
			☐	☐	
			☐	☐	
			☐	☐	
			☐	☐	
			☐	☐	

TOTAL PAID: _____ **TOTAL DUE:** _____

Notes / Unexpected Expenses:

_____

_____

_____

_____

_____

_____

Reflections

monthly Review

DOES MY INCOME AND DEBT ADD UP

_____

_____

_____

HOW CAN I MAKE NEXT MONTH BETTER

_____

_____

WHAT DID I LEARN THIS MONTH ABOUT MY
SPENDING

_____

_____

_____

DO I NEED TO ADJUST
SPENDING LIMITS

_____

_____

_____

DID MEET THIS MONTH'S
GOALS

INCOME

Month:

Date	Source	Expected	Actual
		TOTAL	

Side Hustle

OTHER INCOME

Date	Source	Expected	Actual
		TOTAL	

Monthly Budget  Planner

<<<<<

Total Income	

BILLS TO BE PAID	BUDGET	ACTUAL	DIFFERENCE	BILL DUE DATE/NOTES
Budget is balance when Income - Expenses = Zero				
Rent/Mortgage				
Car Payment				
Car Insurance				
Electricity				
Cables				
Gas				
Phone				

>>>>>

TOTAL BUDGETED	

Other Expenses Budget

Other Expenses and Subscriptions

EXPENSES	BUDGET	ACTUAL	DIFFERENCE	BILL DUE DATE/NOTES

MONTHLY BUDGET SAVINGS GOALS

TOTAL BUDGETED

FUND	BUDGET	ACTUAL
Emergency Fund		
Investment		
Savings		
Auto Repair		

TOTAL BUDGETED

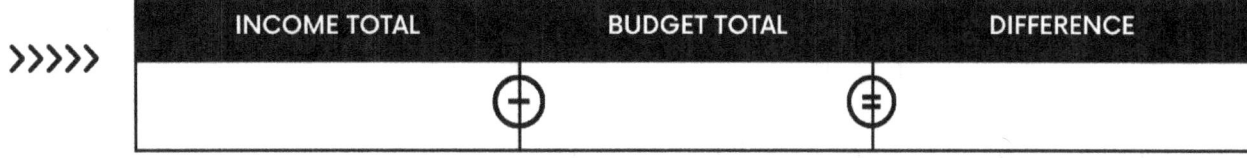

	INCOME TOTAL	BUDGET TOTAL	DIFFERENCE
>>>>>	⊕	⊜	

Balance Budget

Monthly Spending  Tracker

Date	Description	Category	Amount
		Total	

monthly Overview

Sunday	Monday	Tuesday	Wednesday	Thursday	Friday	Saturday

⟶ WHAT ARE MY FINANCIAL
PRIORITIES THIS MONTH

⟶ WHAT IS MY SELF-CARE
GOAL THIS MONTH

My finances don't scare me because I have a plan

WEEKLY PLANNER

Monday

Tuesday

Wednesday

Thursday

Friday

Saturday

Sunday

GOALS

AFFIRMATION

Meal Planner
STAY ON BUDGET

NOTES

Bill Payment

Weekly Income:

Week of:

This Week Bills Due / Paid Date	Amount Owe	Amount Paid	Full Payment	Partial Payment	Balance Due

TOTAL PAID:		**TOTAL DUE:**

Notes / Unexpected Expenses:

_____

_____

_____   _____

_____   _____

_____   _____

_____   _____

_____   _____

_____

WEEKLY PLANNER

Monday

Tuesday

Wednesday

Thursday

Friday

Saturday

Sunday

GOALS

AFFIRMATION

Meal Planner

STAY ON BUDGET

NOTES

Bill Payment

Weekly Income:

Week of:

This Week Bills Due / Paid Date	Amount Owe	Amount Paid	Full Payment	Partial Payment	Balance Due
			☐	☐	
			☐	☐	
			☐	☐	
			☐	☐	
			☐	☐	
			☐	☐	
			☐	☐	
			☐	☐	
			☐	☐	
			☐	☐	
			☐	☐	

TOTAL PAID: **TOTAL DUE:**

Notes / Unexpected Expenses:

WEEKLY PLANNER

Monday

Tuesday

Wednesday

Thursday

Friday

Saturday

Sunday

GOALS

AFFIRMATION

Meal Planner

STAY ON BUDGET

NOTES

Bill Payment

Weekly Income:

Week of:

This Week Bills Due / Paid Date	Amount Owe	Amount Paid	Full Payment	Partial Payment	Balance Due
			☐	☐	
			☐	☐	
			☐	☐	
			☐	☐	
			☐	☐	
			☐	☐	
			☐	☐	
			☐	☐	
			☐	☐	
			☐	☐	
			☐	☐	

TOTAL PAID: ____ **TOTAL DUE:** ____

Notes / Unexpected Expenses:

_____

_____

_____ _____

_____ _____

_____ _____

_____ _____

_____ _____

WEEKLY PLANNER

Monday

Tuesday

Wednesday

Thursday

Friday

Saturday

Sunday

GOALS

AFFIRMATION

Meal Planner
STAY ON BUDGET

NOTES

Bill Payment

Weekly Income:

Week of: _____

This Week Bills Due / Paid Date	Amount Owe	Amount Paid	Full Payment	Partial Payment	Balance Due
			☐	☐	
			☐	☐	
			☐	☐	
			☐	☐	
			☐	☐	
			☐	☐	
			☐	☐	
			☐	☐	
			☐	☐	
			☐	☐	
			☐	☐	
TOTAL PAID:			**TOTAL DUE:**		

Notes / Unexpected Expenses:

_____

_____

_____   _____

_____   _____

_____   _____

_____   _____

_____   _____

Reflections

monthly Review

DOES MY INCOME AND DEBT ADD UP

_____

_____

_____

HOW CAN I MAKE NEXT MONTH BETTER

_____

_____

WHAT DID I LEARN THIS MONTH ABOUT MY
SPENDING

_____

_____

_____

DO I NEED TO ADJUST
SPENDING LIMITS

_____

_____

_____

DID MEET THIS MONTH'S
GOALS

INCOME

Month:

Date	Source	Expected	Actual
		TOTAL	

Side Hustle

OTHER INCOME

Date	Source	Expected	Actual
		TOTAL	

Monthly Budget Planner

<<<<<

Total Income	

BILLS TO BE PAID	BUDGET	ACTUAL	DIFFERENCE	BILL DUE DATE/NOTES
Budget is balance when Income - Expenses = Zero				
Rent/Mortgage				
Car Payment				
Car Insurance				
Electricity				
Cables				
Gas				
Phone				

>>>>>

TOTAL BUDGETED	

Other Expenses Budget

<<<<<

Budget for your Lifestyle

Other Expenses and Subscriptions

EXPENSES	BUDGET	ACTUAL	DIFFERENCE	BILL DUE DATE/NOTES

TOTAL BUDGETED	

MONTHLY BUDGET SAVINGS GOALS

FUND	BUDGET	ACTUAL
Emergency Fund		
Investment		
Savings		
Auto Repair		

TOTAL BUDGETED	

Balance Budget

>>>>>

INCOME TOTAL	BUDGET TOTAL	DIFFERENCE
⊕	⊜	

Monthly Spending Tracker

Date	Description	Category	Amount
		Total	

monthly Overview

Sunday	Monday	Tuesday	Wednesday	Thursday	Friday	Saturday

⟶ **WHAT ARE MY FINANCIAL PRIORITIES THIS MONTH**

⟶ **WHAT IS MY SELF-CARE GOAL THIS MONTH**

My finances don't scare me because I have a plan

WEEKLY PLANNER

Monday

Tuesday

Wednesday

Thursday

Friday

Saturday

Sunday

GOALS

AFFIRMATION

Meal Planner

STAY ON BUDGET

NOTES

Bill Payment

Weekly Income:

Week of: _____

This Week Bills Due / Paid Date	Amount Owe	Amount Paid	Full Payment	Partial Payment	Balance Due
			☐	☐	
			☐	☐	
			☐	☐	
			☐	☐	
			☐	☐	
			☐	☐	
			☐	☐	
			☐	☐	
			☐	☐	
			☐	☐	
			☐	☐	

TOTAL PAID: _____ **TOTAL DUE:** _____

Notes / Unexpected Expenses:

_____

_____

_____ _____

_____ _____

_____ _____

_____ _____

_____ _____

WEEKLY PLANNER

Monday

Tuesday

Wednesday

Thursday

Friday

Saturday

Sunday

GOALS

AFFIRMATION

Meal Planner
STAY ON BUDGET

NOTES

Bill Payment

Weekly Income:

Week of:

This Week Bills Due / Paid Date	Amount Owe	Amount Paid	Full Payment	Partial Payment	Balance Due
			☐	☐	
			☐	☐	
			☐	☐	
			☐	☐	
			☐	☐	
			☐	☐	
			☐	☐	
			☐	☐	
			☐	☐	
			☐	☐	
			☐	☐	

TOTAL PAID: | | **TOTAL DUE:** |

Notes / Unexpected Expenses:

WEEKLY PLANNER

Monday

Tuesday

Wednesday

Thursday

Friday

Saturday

Sunday

GOALS

AFFIRMATION

Meal Planner
STAY ON BUDGET

NOTES

Bill Payment

Weekly Income:

Week of: _____

This Week Bills Due / Paid Date	Amount Owe	Amount Paid	Full Payment	Partial Payment	Balance Due
			▢	▢	
			▢	▢	
			▢	▢	
			▢	▢	
			▢	▢	
			▢	▢	
			▢	▢	
			▢	▢	
			▢	▢	
			▢	▢	
			▢	▢	

TOTAL PAID: _____   **TOTAL DUE:** _____

Notes / Unexpected Expenses:

_____

_____

_____   _____

_____   _____

_____   _____

_____   _____

_____

WEEKLY PLANNER

Monday

Tuesday

Wednesday

Thursday

Friday

Saturday

Sunday

GOALS

AFFIRMATION

Meal Planner

STAY ON BUDGET

NOTES

Bill Payment

Weekly Income:

Week of:

This Week Bills Due / Paid Date	Amount Owe	Amount Paid	Full Payment	Partial Payment	Balance Due
			☐	☐	
			☐	☐	
			☐	☐	
			☐	☐	
			☐	☐	
			☐	☐	
			☐	☐	
			☐	☐	
			☐	☐	
			☐	☐	
			☐	☐	
	TOTAL PAID:			TOTAL DUE:	

Notes / Unexpected Expenses:

_____

_____

_____   _____

_____   _____

_____   _____

_____   _____

Reflections

monthly Review

DOES MY INCOME AND DEBT ADD UP

_____

_____

_____

HOW CAN I MAKE NEXT MONTH BETTER

_____

_____

WHAT DID I LEARN THIS MONTH ABOUT MY
SPENDING

_____

_____

_____

DO I NEED TO ADJUST
SPENDING LIMITS

_____

_____

_____

DID MEET THIS MONTH'S
GOALS

INCOME

Month:

Date	Source	Expected	Actual
		TOTAL	

Side Hustle

OTHER INCOME

Date	Source	Expected	Actual
		TOTAL	

Monthly Budget Planner

<<<<<

Total Income	

BILLS TO BE PAID	BUDGET	ACTUAL	DIFFERENCE	BILL DUE DATE/NOTES
Budget is balance when Income - Expenses = Zero				
Rent/Mortgage				
Car Payment				
Car Insurance				
Electricity				
Cables				
Gas				
Phone				

>>>>>

TOTAL BUDGETED	

Other Expenses Budget

Other Expenses and Subscriptions

EXPENSES	BUDGET	ACTUAL	DIFFERENCE	BILL DUE DATE/NOTES

TOTAL BUDGETED

MONTHLY BUDGET SAVINGS GOALS

FUND	BUDGET	ACTUAL
Emergency Fund		
Investment		
Savings		
Auto Repair		

TOTAL BUDGETED

Balance Budget

INCOME TOTAL	BUDGET TOTAL	DIFFERENCE
⊕	⊜	

>>>>>

Monthly Spending  Tracker

Date	Description	Category	Amount
		Total	

CALENDAR

monthly Overview

Sunday	Monday	Tuesday	Wednesday	Thursday	Friday	Saturday

⟶ WHAT ARE MY FINANCIAL
PRIORITIES THIS MONTH

⟶ WHAT IS MY SELF-CARE
GOAL THIS MONTH

My finances don't scare me because I have a plan

WEEKLY PLANNER

Monday

Tuesday

Wednesday

Thursday

Friday

Saturday

Sunday

GOALS

AFFIRMATION

Meal Planner

STAY ON BUDGET

NOTES

Bill Payment

Weekly Income:

Week of: _____

This Week Bills Due / Paid Date	Amount Owe	Amount Paid	Full Payment	Partial Payment	Balance Due
			☐	☐	
			☐	☐	
			☐	☐	
			☐	☐	
			☐	☐	
			☐	☐	
			☐	☐	
			☐	☐	
			☐	☐	
			☐	☐	
			☐	☐	

TOTAL PAID: _____   **TOTAL DUE:** _____

Notes / Unexpected Expenses:

_____ _____

_____ _____

_____ _____

_____ _____

_____ _____

WEEKLY PLANNER

Monday

Tuesday

Wednesday

Thursday

Friday

Saturday

Sunday

GOALS

AFFIRMATION

Meal Planner

STAY ON BUDGET

NOTES

Bill Payment

Weekly Income:

Week of:

This Week Bills Due / Paid Date	Amount Owe	Amount Paid	Full Payment	Partial Payment	Balance Due
			▢	▢	
			▢	▢	
			▢	▢	
			▢	▢	
			▢	▢	
			▢	▢	
			▢	▢	
			▢	▢	
			▢	▢	
			▢	▢	
			▢	▢	

TOTAL PAID: | | **TOTAL DUE:** |

Notes / Unexpected Expenses:

WEEKLY PLANNER

Monday

Tuesday

Wednesday

Thursday

Friday

Saturday

Sunday

GOALS

AFFIRMATION

Meal Planner

STAY ON BUDGET

NOTES

Weekly Income:

Bill Payment

Week of:

This Week Bills Due / Paid Date	Amount Owe	Amount Paid	Full Payment	Partial Payment	Balance Due
			▢	▢	
			▢	▢	
			▢	▢	
			▢	▢	
			▢	▢	
			▢	▢	
			▢	▢	
			▢	▢	
			▢	▢	
			▢	▢	
			▢	▢	

TOTAL PAID: **TOTAL DUE:**

Notes / Unexpected Expenses:

_____

_____

_____ _____

_____ _____

_____ _____

_____ _____

WEEKLY PLANNER

Monday

Tuesday

Wednesday

Thursday

Friday

Saturday

Sunday

GOALS

AFFIRMATION

Meal Planner
STAY ON BUDGET

NOTES

Weekly Income:

Bill Payment

Week of: _____

This Week Bills Due / Paid Date	Amount Owe	Amount Paid	Full Payment	Partial Payment	Balance Due
			▢	▢	
			▢	▢	
			▢	▢	
			▢	▢	
			▢	▢	
			▢	▢	
			▢	▢	
			▢	▢	
			▢	▢	
			▢	▢	
			▢	▢	

TOTAL PAID: _____   **TOTAL DUE:** _____

Notes / Unexpected Expenses:

_____

_____

_____   _____

_____   _____

_____   _____

_____   _____

_____

Reflections

monthly Review

DOES MY INCOME AND DEBT ADD UP

_____

_____

_____

HOW CAN I MAKE NEXT MONTH BETTER

_____

_____

WHAT DID I LEARN THIS MONTH ABOUT MY SPENDING

_____

_____

_____

DO I NEED TO ADJUST SPENDING LIMITS

_____

_____

_____

DID MEET THIS MONTH'S GOALS

INCOME

Month:

Date	Source	Expected	Actual
		TOTAL	

Side Hustle

OTHER INCOME

Date	Source	Expected	Actual
		TOTAL	

Monthly Budget *Planner*

Total Income	

BILLS TO BE PAID	BUDGET	ACTUAL	DIFFERENCE	BILL DUE DATE/NOTES
Budget is balance when Income - Expenses = Zero				
Rent/Mortgage				
Car Payment				
Car Insurance				
Electricity				
Cables				
Gas				
Phone				

>>>>>

TOTAL BUDGETED	

Other Expenses Budget

Other Expenses and Subscriptions

EXPENSES	BUDGET	ACTUAL	DIFFERENCE	BILL DUE DATE/NOTES

TOTAL BUDGETED

MONTHLY BUDGET SAVINGS GOALS

FUND	BUDGET	ACTUAL
Emergency Fund		
Investment		
Savings		
Auto Repair		

TOTAL BUDGETED

Balance Budget

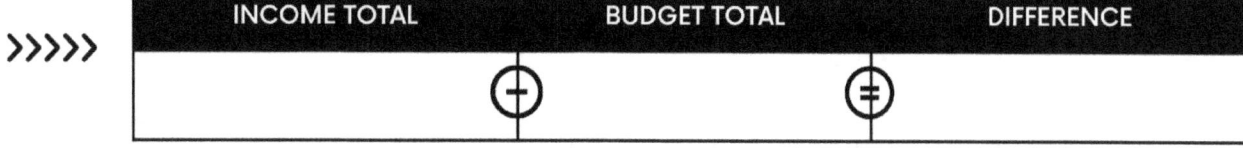

INCOME TOTAL	BUDGET TOTAL	DIFFERENCE
⊕	⊜	

»»»

Monthly Spending *Tracker*

Date	Description	Category	Amount
		Total	

CALENDAR

monthly Overview

Sunday	Monday	Tuesday	Wednesday	Thursday	Friday	Saturday

→ WHAT ARE MY FINANCIAL PRIORITIES THIS MONTH

→ WHAT IS MY SELF-CARE GOAL THIS MONTH

My finances don't scare me because I have a plan

WEEKLY PLANNER

Monday

Tuesday

Wednesday

Thursday

Friday

Saturday

Sunday

GOALS

AFFIRMATION

Meal Planner
STAY ON BUDGET

NOTES

Bill Payment

Weekly Income:

Week of:

This Week Bills Due / Paid Date	Amount Owe	Amount Paid	Full Payment	Partial Payment	Balance Due
			☐	☐	
			☐	☐	
			☐	☐	
			☐	☐	
			☐	☐	
			☐	☐	
			☐	☐	
			☐	☐	
			☐	☐	
			☐	☐	
			☐	☐	

TOTAL PAID: **TOTAL DUE:**

Notes / Unexpected Expenses:

WEEKLY PLANNER

Monday

Tuesday

Wednesday

Thursday

Friday

Saturday

Sunday

GOALS

AFFIRMATION

Meal Planner

STAY ON BUDGET

NOTES

Bill Payment

Weekly Income:

Week of: _____

This Week Bills Due / Paid Date	Amount Owe	Amount Paid	Full Payment	Partial Payment	Balance Due
			☐	☐	
			☐	☐	
			☐	☐	
			☐	☐	
			☐	☐	
			☐	☐	
			☐	☐	
			☐	☐	
			☐	☐	
			☐	☐	
			☐	☐	

TOTAL PAID: _____ **TOTAL DUE:** _____

Notes / Unexpected Expenses:

_____

_____

_____ _____

_____ _____

_____ _____

_____ _____

WEEKLY PLANNER

Monday

Tuesday

Wednesday

Thursday

Friday

Saturday

Sunday

GOALS

AFFIRMATION

Meal Planner

STAY ON BUDGET

NOTES

Weekly Income:

Bill Payment

Week of: _____

This Week Bills Due / Paid Date	Amount Owe	Amount Paid	Full Payment	Partial Payment	Balance Due
			☐	☐	
			☐	☐	
			☐	☐	
			☐	☐	
			☐	☐	
			☐	☐	
			☐	☐	
			☐	☐	
			☐	☐	
			☐	☐	
			☐	☐	

TOTAL PAID:		TOTAL DUE:	

Notes / Unexpected Expenses:

_____

_____

_____ _____

_____ _____

_____ _____

_____ _____

_____

WEEKLY PLANNER

Monday

Tuesday

Wednesday

Thursday

Friday

Saturday

Sunday

GOALS

AFFIRMATION

Meal Planner

STAY ON BUDGET

NOTES

Bill Payment

Weekly Income:

Week of:

This Week Bills Due / Paid Date	Amount Owe	Amount Paid	Full Payment	Partial Payment	Balance Due
			☐	☐	
			☐	☐	
			☐	☐	
			☐	☐	
			☐	☐	
			☐	☐	
			☐	☐	
			☐	☐	
			☐	☐	
			☐	☐	
			☐	☐	

TOTAL PAID: **TOTAL DUE:**

Notes / Unexpected Expenses:

Reflections

monthly Review

DOES MY INCOME AND DEBT ADD UP

_____

_____

_____

HOW CAN I MAKE NEXT MONTH BETTER

_____

_____

WHAT DID I LEARN THIS MONTH ABOUT MY SPENDING

_____

_____

_____

DO I NEED TO ADJUST SPENDING LIMITS

_____

_____

_____

DID MEET THIS MONTH'S GOALS

Subscription Tracker

Date	Bill	Amount	Frequency		Auto Renew
			Monthly	Yearly	
			☐	☐	
			☐	☐	
			☐	☐	
			☐	☐	
			☐	☐	
			☐	☐	
			☐	☐	
			☐	☐	
			☐	☐	
			☐	☐	
			☐	☐	
			☐	☐	
			☐	☐	
			☐	☐	
			☐	☐	
			☐	☐	
			☐	☐	
			☐	☐	
			☐	☐	

FINANCIAL JOURNAL

FINANCIAL JOURNAL

FINANCIAL JOURNAL

Savings Fund

Fund Name	Goal Amount

Notes:

Starting Amount:

Per/Week :   Per/Month :

Due Date :

JAN	FEB	MAR	APR	MAY	JUN

JUL	AUG	SEPT	OCT	NOV	DEC

Savings Fund

Fund Name	Goal Amount

Notes:

Starting Amount:

Per/Week :   Per/Month :

Due Date :

JAN	FEB	MAR	APR	MAY	JUN

JUL	AUG	SEPT	OCT	NOV	DEC

Savings Fund

Fund Name	Goal Amount

Notes:

Starting Amount:

Per/Week :   Per/Month :

Due Date :

JAN	FEB	MAR	APR	MAY	JUN

JUL	AUG	SEPT	OCT	NOV	DEC

DEBT SNOWBALL
TRACKER

THE DEBT SNOWBALL METHOD IS A DEBT-REDUCTION STRATEGY, WHEREBY ONE WHO OWES ON MORE THAN ONE ACCOUNT PAYS OFF THE ACCOUNTS STARTING WITH THE SMALLEST BALANCES FIRST, WHILE PAYING THE MINIMUM PAYMENT ON LARGER DEBTS.

	DEBT	TOTAL AMOUNT DUE	MINIMUM PAYMENT	DEBT SNOWBALL PAYMENT
JAN				
FEB				
MAR				
APR				
MAY				
JUN				
JUL				
AUG				
SEP				
OCT				
NOV				
DEC				

DEBT SNOWBALL

Tracker

THE DEBT SNOWBALL METHOD IS A DEBT-REDUCTION STRATEGY, WHEREBY ONE WHO OWES ON MORE THAN ONE ACCOUNT PAYS OFF THE ACCOUNTS STARTING WITH THE SMALLEST BALANCES FIRST, WHILE PAYING THE MINIMUM PAYMENT ON LARGER DEBTS.

	DEBT	TOTAL AMOUNT DUE	MINIMUM PAYMENT	DEBT SNOWBALL PAYMENT
JAN				
FEB				
MAR				
APR				
MAY				
JUN				
JUL				
AUG				
SEP				
OCT				
NOV				
DEC				

DEBT SNOWBALL
Tracker

THE DEBT SNOWBALL METHOD IS A DEBT-REDUCTION STRATEGY, WHEREBY ONE WHO OWES ON MORE THAN ONE ACCOUNT PAYS OFF THE ACCOUNTS STARTING WITH THE SMALLEST BALANCES FIRST, WHILE PAYING THE MINIMUM PAYMENT ON LARGER DEBTS.

	DEBT	TOTAL AMOUNT DUE	MINIMUM PAYMENT	DEBT SNOWBALL PAYMENT
JAN				
FEB				
MAR				
APR				
MAY				
JUN				
JUL				
AUG				
SEP				
OCT				
NOV				
DEC				

DEBT SNOWBALL

THE DEBT SNOWBALL METHOD IS A DEBT-REDUCTION STRATEGY, WHEREBY ONE WHO OWES ON MORE THAN ONE ACCOUNT PAYS OFF THE ACCOUNTS STARTING WITH THE SMALLEST BALANCES FIRST, WHILE PAYING THE MINIMUM PAYMENT ON LARGER DEBTS.

	DEBT	TOTAL AMOUNT DUE	MINIMUM PAYMENT	DEBT SNOWBALL PAYMENT
JAN				
FEB				
MAR				
APR				
MAY				
JUN				
JUL				
AUG				
SEP				
OCT				
NOV				
DEC				

www.ingramcontent.com/pod-product-compliance
Lightning Source LLC
Chambersburg PA
CBHW082146120626
46553CB00010B/2784